HeartPeace

HeartPeace

Healing Help for Grieving Folks

by Richard B. Gilbert

Abbey Press
St. Meinrad, IN 47577

© 1996 Richard B. Gilbert
Published by One Caring Place
Abbey Press
St. Meinrad, IN 47577

Library of Congress Catalog Number
96-85874
ISBN 0-87029-298-6

Book design by Scott Wannemuehler
Cover design by Michael O'Neill McGrath, OSFS

Printed in the United States of America

In Loving Memory

Helen Cairney (Gram)
Eleanor T. Gilbert
Frederic B. Gilbert, III
Austin Sims
Esther Lutze
Ann Parks
John Drennan
Barbara Thompson
Lucille Weidner
Our Unborn Child

Foreword

A long time ago, a young mother cried out in despair, raising her empty arms heavenward, seeking an answer to her grief. She knew her cries of anguish went unheard by a God she no longer believed in. If God had been listening, surely the young mother would not now be drowning in such sorrow! If only God had not been busy answering someone else's prayers; if only she had been "better" or more faithful; if only she had prayed longer or louder or differently—*if only* rang through her soul and she knew she was alone in her despair. Her prayers had gone unanswered and she turned away from the heavens, grieving now not only the death of her child, but the death of her religion and faith as well.

I was that mother. When our son, Austin, died of a malignant brain tumor, he took with him all our hopes and dreams, our faith and our joy. There were no happy sounds in our house anymore and the sun cast only shadows of sadness. Joy had been buried one afternoon in late fall, and winter came to reside within our hearts. Would we ever be happy again? Would I ever laugh or dream or sing again?

How I wish I had known Dick Gilbert then! How I wish we could have experienced his compassion, his understanding, his faith. We were so lost and confused. We stumbled through the Valley of the Shadow, grieving not only the death of our son, but the loss of close friendships, self-esteem, self-identity, and faith as well. If only we had been able to read his words. I needed a book such a Dick's! I am thankful for it now.

I don't know how Dick Gilbert knows my pain and despair, but somehow he understands the loneliness of not only grieving the death of a loved one, but the terrible despair of losing one's faith as well. He understands the confusion and pain of being bereaved and has given us a book of hope for the journey.

Dick speaks so clearly of our need for connections—to our pain, to our loved one no longer within hug's reach, to each other, and to ourselves. He gently invites us to give our faith another chance and provides us with a better understanding of the differences between religion and spirituality. He asks only that we honor and respect our pain as we search for the connections we so desperately seek.

We may feel like scattered pieces of a broken puzzle, but Dick suggests that perhaps the pieces can be rearranged, reshuffled, and pieced together again to form a different picture. With Dick's clear guidance, the bereaved can begin to understand that "healing is not about forgetting, but remembering."

Dick's book becomes an invitation to connect the broken pieces, to reconnect to our sense of self, to our family, and to our God. He provides the "glue" that helps mend the ragged edges and gently guides the hurting soul home.

The human spirit has an infinite capacity to endure, survive, and grow. It requires laughter and tears to flourish. It requires love and faith, strength and support as well. Hurt and pain have their lessons, and we cannot rob ourselves of the richness of the tapestry that hurt and love weave together. To eliminate one from the loom is to break the thread and steal away the fabric.

The gifts within love are obvious. We do not dispute them. Yet the gifts within hurt are equally real. I could not understand light if I had not known darkness. I could not sing sweet if I had not tasted bitter. I could not laugh if I had not cried.

Dick Gilbert's book is a gift of hope to those who have lost their way in their despair. It is a gift of hope to all who have ever searched the heavens for answers and believed they were not heard. Dick invites the grieving to reconnect and to find the hope that lies within each of us. I thank God for the gift of Dick Gilbert and the light he shines in the darkness of grief.

Peace be with you as you seek the connections that will heal the hurting spaces. May love be what you remember the most.

—*Darcie D. Sims. Ph.D., CGC, CHT*

Preface

Gram was one classy lady. She had a regal splendor about her that just breathed elegance and charm. She looked like the "Queen Mum," dressed with that same air of style—she wouldn't think of going to church without a hat and even came to breakfast well dressed. She had style, she had charm, and she was to me a mother, confidante, and best friend. She died a few days before I finished seminary in 1970 and still is a vital energy and presence in my life.

Gram loved to play games, especially *Scrabble*. I still have the last score sheet from our series that ran from high school to seminary. The final tally of games was 104-89 in her favor. That's a lot of *Scrabble*! We were good at it (though she was obviously much better). In those days in New York City we had at least seven daily newspapers, and Gram did the crossword puzzles in all of them. She looked for the complicated word. I looked for the triple word score.

One day we began to discover a shortcut to resetting all of the *Scrabble* tiles. We pushed them all to one side of the board, crowded together, faceup. We put the box lid over the letters, grabbed the lid and the bottom of the game board, flipped it over and—*voila*—all the tiles were now facedown and ready for the next game. We had invented something. After seeing this work to perfection more times than we could count, we called in Uncle Bob and my father to watch the miraculous discovery.

We built it up with great dramatic effect. Gram did her thing, but disaster struck and we had what seemed to be hundreds of little tiles all over the living room floor. Uncle Bob and my father were not amused. (I don't know whether they were more annoyed that we wasted their time or that we would waste our own time with *Scrabble*.) We just laughed and picked up tiles. We played several games without the "demon *Q*" until we discovered it while dusting a heating vent.

That story has never left me because it has been the story that has helped me experience and, to some extent, understand Gram's death, and all of the deaths (and other challenges) in my life. *Experience*, yes. *Understand?* Occasionally. Death is about flipping (or being flipped by) the game board of life and having the tiles (the pieces of our life) thrown all over the living room, the house, the neighborhood, the world. We are shattered and scattered, like ashes in the breeze, and there is no hope of life again. Death takes the smooth operation of life, the understandable or manageable story, and shreds it all to pieces. We desperately search for something or someone to pull the pieces together, to bring some wholeness out of brokenness that seems beyond recognition and repair.

Gram was a devout woman, a woman who breathed and believed the faith she shared in very simple ways. In many ways she was my call to the ministry. That fact seemed to make little difference as the halls of Trinity Lutheran Seminary were shattered by the wailing of my broken heart when Gram died. I knew then, as I know now, that nothing would ever be the same again.

This book is about grief, about experiencing loss. It is about life. This book is not about answers (the bereaved quickly discover there are no answers), but about the connection of the spiritual that brings peace out of pieces, and helps us stay connected even when we are shattered and scattered.

This book is about the thousands of stories I have been privileged to encounter and hear through many speeches, lectures, workshops, hallway conversations, phone calls, and the letters I have received from all over the world. These are the stories of bereaved parents, hurting siblings, overloaded caregivers, wounded spouses—all the people whose lives have been ripped apart by a death. It is offered not by a preacher who foolishly believes that the right words will work this all out. It is offered by a wounded and bereaved parent and bereavement specialist—not out of my understanding but out of the experience of staying connected when I believed I would be disconnected forever.

I will not preach at you. That is never my style. You do not have to agree with my spirituality. Everyone is spiritual, however that is defined, and it is *your* spirituality that will be the pathway or connection for *your* healing. This spirituality is not an afterthought, or one other possible way of getting through this grief. It is the ultimate way, the final way, the one piece of a very disrupted life that will lead you to peace.

Is this a grief book? Yes. Is it a book about spirituality? Yes.

That is the point. To face grief without access to our spiritual resources is an incomplete journey. To wrestle with spiritual issues apart from our struggles with loss is to remove the vital energy of our faith system from the very human experiences that cry out for that important connection.

This book was not created in my study. It was written in the trenches of hospital rooms, little family rooms in the emergency room, support groups, and in the presence of the faces and words of thousands of bereaved folks I have been privileged to meet and listen to. I thank all of them for sharing. The pain for them was tremendous. At times I felt both helpless and useless, jarred into the pain of my own losses and questions, as together we struggled to claim a connectedness that hinted at one tiny step forward to healing. My thanks to *all* of you.

Thank you, too, to the many very special people (I can't possibly remember or name them all) who cared for me, who taught me, who demanded that I write this book, who affirmed what I was struggling to understand and express to others. A big Thank You to Darcie and Tony Sims, Allie (Sims) Franklin, Rabbi Earl Grollman, Andrea Gambill, Glen Davidson, Patrick DelZoppo, Sr. Jane Marie Lamb, John (Jack) Morgan, Tom Droege, Jim Miller, Dale Guckenberger, Paul Alexander, Chaplains Harold ter Blanche and Pam Russell in Great Britain, Doug and Barbara Manning, Mickey McGrath, Leo Booth, Joy and Marv Johnson, and the Centering Corporation family, Sherry Williams and the family at ACCORD, my many clergy and chaplain colleagues and friends, especially Gary Sproat and Rob Shores—and all of those very special folks helping others along the road of grief.

There are many others whose stories leap in my heart. I thank you, too. A big hug (hugs are important to the bereaved) to the many "families" who have added to this book—Hope For Bereaved, Abbey Press/CareNotes, The Compassionate Friends (United States and United Kingdom), The National Catholic Ministry to the Bereaved (from a grateful Lutheran), SHARE, In Loving Memory, Alive Alone, and The College of Chaplains. I say thank you to the folks at the two hospitals (Iowa and Indiana) where I was privileged to work on my grief agenda with very special patients, their loved ones, physicians, and other colleagues.

Finally, a very special thank you to my lovely wife, Sharon, my daughter, Allison, and in memory of the unnamed child we were not allowed to know. Sharon and Allison have taught me so much about my own grief journey, not with words but with embraces, tears, smiles, and nudges to keep going, to stay with myself, with my God, with my journey—even when I felt like I was experiencing another dead end. They always seemed to understand why I had to buy "just a few more books," or go on the road to another course or conference. They didn't object, at least not too much, when I stayed up late to write another review, got out of bed for what seemed like the hundredth time to respond to the beeper, or when one more dinner or outing was interrupted by someone who needed to talk.

From pieces to peace. Why is life such a rough ride? Why does grief feel so impossible? Why do you often seem so far away, God? Why? Why? Why? These are the questions of grief, and they are the questions of my spiritual journey.

Help us, Lord, to see that it is your love, your embrace (which right now may feel very absent) that becomes the binding glue, the stroke of the artist's brush, that pulls together all of the shattered pieces in our lives and paints the possibility of a new horizon of hope. Amen.

—*Dick Gilbert*

12

Glossary

Before getting further into the book, I need to define some words we will be using. These words are crucial to the book. It is equally crucial for you to understand that this book is committed to your right to have your own definitions of these words. The essence of the book is not that we agree on terms, but that you claim your own spiritual pathway to healing.

GOD—I am Christian and worship with Lutheran and Episcopalian leanings. I believe in an empowering, loving, actively present God, revealed to me in Jesus, who continues to be present decisively in the world and in my life. You may believe in God as a Jew, as a Muslim, through another faith system, or in your own way. You may only be able to speak of Higher Power or some Eternal Being or Source beyond your own life. You may believe that there is no God or divine power at all. *Don't throw the book away.* You still have your spirituality, and it is still your pathway to healing.

SPIRITUALITY and *RELIGION*—People use these words interchangeably, *but they are not the same thing.* Simply put, spirituality is the expression of relationship or connection with God as you know God. It is the "I" of that relationship. It is where we find our strength and, in times of loss, where we can find ourselves to be the most wounded. Religion is the "We," how we bring our spiritual awareness into some kind of community. Religion is community, denomination, doctrine—the formalization of our spirituality as we interact with others. The two are often so interrelated that we cannot separate them, but please remember that they are not the same. We will have much more to say about these words.

CHURCH—This is a very specific term in the Christian community. It means a specific congregation or religious community and the whole Christian community as the People of God or Body of Christ. When we use this word, or the word *congregation*, we are speaking of a religious community, whatever its context or belief system. We are speaking of the people and community you turn to when you seek to define your spirituality and seek comfort and understanding. It is where the individual believer goes to find fam-

13

ily, the experience of community support, and mutual concern.

God of love, I sometimes feel lost. Even words easily defined can become new detours, more challenges than I care to bear. Help me to see that you are my focus, and that you are the magnet that draws me to yourself.

Help us to realize that even when we feel out of focus, you are ever focused on us. Amen.

Last Things

"Two outs, bottom of the ninth." "Three seconds left on the shot clock." "Do they have time for one more play?" "She seems ready to breathe her last." We understand and experience many "last things" in our lives. Life is filled with lasts, just as it is filled with firsts.

Death is about lasts, or at least it seems that way. It starts there because a life, an experience, has been shattered. The *Scrabble* pieces of our lives are ripped apart and thrown all over (the devastating winds of a tornado or hurricane are probably closer to the truth!). The death of a loved one, of a relationship, of a marriage, of a dream, are experiences of an ending, or many endings, and we are shattered and scattered as we hopelessly try to fit the pieces of our lives back together again.

We can't do it, though. We can't put the pieces back together again. To do that is to think that, somehow, with the right hard work, by reading the right book, by attending the right support group, or finding the right "glue," we can take all those scattered tiles of our story and put them back together again. Only after time do we learn the hardest lesson—that nothing will ever be the same again. You can play 100 games of *Scrabble* and not use the same letters twice. There is only one Z, one J, one X, and one Q (the nasty demons that I always get too late in the game), but the finished game boards and the words used are different in every game.

Healing, however, is a creation, not recreation, and we have to get through the last or final things to get there. For a long time we deny the possibility of healing. It hurts too bad. We are often afraid to heal because we don't understand it. Of course, the hurtful remarks of family and friends ("You should be *over this* by now") don't help. We are confused about healing. We think of it as being done, another last thing, and that feels like forgetting. Who wants to forget (or allow to be forgotten) a loved one? I don't want that kind of "healing" as I deal with my many losses.

Healing is not about forgetting, but *remembering*. When we begin to remember that the person who has died is always with us, instead of remembering that a loved one has died, we are starting to heal. We are getting there, beginning anew, picking up a few more tiles, seeing a hint of the picture in that 5,000-piece puzzle.

We began with endings—last things. For a long time, or what seems like a long time, we can only remember what happened *last:* The *last* kiss, the *last* conversation, the *last* shared cup of coffee, the *last* time we saw our child get on the school bus, the *last* word shared in a hospital room, the *last* breath. When those *lasts* are compromised by unfinished or hurtful words, it takes even longer. We just can't stop remembering the *lasts,* and it seems that all we do is *last* things. We cry more and more. We babble in ways that make no sense. We say the same words over and over again (as our friends and neighbors seem to back further and further away). Then we feel stuck, wondering if life will be shattered for us—forever.

This book is about the "final piece," and it is intended to help us move through our journey, however slowly, to experience (or believe in the possibility that we will experience) the "final peace." It is not, however, about pieces, even though we may feel shattered and scattered. This book is about the one piece of the puzzle, the one letter or tile, that pulls everything together. It is about finding the key that unlocks our story, validates our feelings, and gives a hint or sense of meaning to that which is absolutely meaningless, or so painful that there can be no meaning or purpose.

We are moving our thoughts to *last,* not *lasts,* to that experience or resource which is last. (Please stay with me. I am not trying to confuse you with theological babble.) *Last* here does not imply sequence. In other words, if there are ten chapters to your life, we are not bypassing one through nine, and talking about number ten. *Last* is about Ultimates, and *final* is about Finality—about that person, word, source, ethic, or meaning that is as much first as it is last. It is equally at home in chapter one, two, three, four as it is in nine and ten. It is the connection in life (watch for the word *connection* throughout this book) that is the story from birth through death. And it is the center of peace, hope, and value even when those qualities seem ripped out of the very fabric of our life by the death of a loved one.

A death, like any loss, makes us the bereaved, and the journey we now walk is called grief. When we are able to grieve, we pour out our feelings, share our story, and move—albeit an inch at a

16

time—to the new beginning of life within those memories. We must release those feelings. This is our only choice—to grieve either in a healthy way or in a manner that cripples us. It is not always easy knowing how to make that choice.

So we search for understanding and meaning. Sometimes we even believe that if someone would just explain all of this it would make sense and everything would be fine. This isn't about logic but about loss, and the way through it is to pour forth all of those feelings. The meaning comes not through our understanding, but through the powerful embrace of spirit (or Spirit). This embrace binds us together as individuals, and keeps us connected (even when it seems there isn't a glue strong enough to bind up all the pieces we are in) to the people, experiences, meaning, and hope that really matter. That glue is the final piece that brings us, *in time*, to the final peace. That piece—and that *peace*—is our spirituality.

Spirituality, however we define it, is the spirit that is within us. This book is about helping us define and find for ourselves the spirit that is already in us, healing when it is needed and being open to new possibilities when they are there. Piece. Peace. It *is* possible for you.

I am different, Lord—I am bereaved. Nothing is the same; everything is different. I feel different. People treat me differently. Loss has been thrust upon me. I may even hold you responsible for that loss. I now must grieve, and I crave a word, a hint of hope and healing.

Help us, Lord, to know that you are ever the same, ever constant in our lives. Amen.

Umbrellas and Extension Cords

I don't know who invented the umbrella, but I do know that he or she either never used one or lived in a desert where it really didn't matter. I have never encountered an invention that is so over-rated and so generally useless.

Think about it. What good is an umbrella? I have yet to find one that does what it is supposed to do—keep me dry. By the time I push the button to open it, I have either injured someone or found an umbrella that will not open, opens inside out, or just keeps going into orbit.

I cannot find umbrellas when I need them, and we even have an umbrella stand in the house. Of course, that is another one of those purposeful things that has lost its purpose. We can't use the umbrella stand, because the floor would get wet if we put umbrellas in it. So it is a nice decoration for some antique umbrellas, but the working umbrellas are tucked away in those convenient places that we cannot find! I have donated dozens of umbrellas to floors under restaurant tables, coatracks in churches and meeting rooms, and to the many people who decide to walk off with them.

About the only use I see for umbrellas is as walking sticks on slick pavement, as required attire for gentlemen with briefcases and bowler hats on London sidewalks, or as a modest weapon to grab a taxi from someone else. That's all fine, *but they do not keep you dry!*

Many of us have what I call *umbrella theologies.* Our umbrella fits comfortably in the closet, in good weather, when things in life are going well, when we believe we have everything on course, working as we would want it to. But watch out when the rains come! A natural disaster, an accident, the death of a loved one or friend, a lost job, health problems—what good is that umbrella then?

Scripture is filled with words of promise. "The Lord is my Shepherd, I shall not want" (Psalm 23:1); "I have called you by name, you are mine" (Isaiah 43:1); "And remember, I am with you always" (Matthew 28:20). Those promises are true, but they are not intended to provide umbrellas of protection from life's pain. Scripture speaks clearly of our mortality. We will die. Depending on the circumstances, when the cause of death challenges us even more, our umbrellas are less and less helpful.

"I am baptized." "I am saved." "I pray every day." "I attend church every Sunday." These statements can lead us to believe that we are protected from harm's way. But when bad things happen, we are faced with questions that reveal the inadequacies of our umbrella theology: "Why did God let her die now?" "Where was God when the drunk driver killed my son?" "If God is a loving God, why do I have cancer?" These struggles are not helped at all by folks who throw in, "It's God's will."

When I try to use an umbrella, it lasts fifteen minutes and I either fold it up or throw it away, if it hasn't blown away already. If you have an umbrella theology, and now are seeking the spiritual connections to heal, you may need to throw away the elements of your theology that are not helpful as you forge a new spirituality.

Healthy spirituality is not about protection *from* death, but about a strength of relationships and an empowerment of faith that stays with us in life *and* in death. Simply put, healthy spirituality equals connections.

The concept came to me from the writing of The Very Reverend Alan Jones, Dean of Grace (Episcopal) Cathedral in San Francisco. His writing shook my weak spiritual foundations. The idea of connections has guided me along a powerful—and very rocky—journey to a depth of faith that doesn't just lead to glorious mountaintops. Mine is a spirituality that says I am equally strengthened in the deepest valleys, the darkest depressions, the roughest losses. This spirituality evolved when I allowed all of that head stuff I had learned to become connected or integrated with my story, my feelings, and with the spiritual peace which is always beyond me, yet within me.

Instead of umbrellas, I use the image of an extension cord. The extension cord is inserted into an outlet that keeps it firmly grounded. The "current" is the endless love and empowering presence of an active, caring, understanding God who stays connected to me (or, actually, I to God) even when the cord is twisted, stepped on, yanked at, or when I feel there is a power outage. The key to my spirituality is that I am always connected and embraced. As I grieve, as I struggle with yet another riddle or unanswered question in life, as I listen to yet another painful story from someone standing in line to talk after a workshop, I watch out for the umbrellas that don't work for me and grab for my connection.

I am connected! I no longer need what I never had—easy answers, things all worked out. The love that is interrupted by a death is too special and too precious for easy answers and quick solutions. It demands the time we call grief and its goal of healing. Umbrellas don't help that. Extension cords do.

We are all on a spiritual journey—an evolving process that is different every morning, and can take various and often new directions in the midst of our deepest valleys and biggest doubts. At times we may only be able to tell ourselves, like a record with a stuck needle, "I am connected, I am connected, I am connected..." And we *are!*

Being connected won't answer your questions, because your questions are unanswerable. These are questions you raise to get the attention of others (including God), to attend to your feelings. The connections will not justify or make right the death of a loved one, for nothing makes it right. But sometimes good things emerge through (or in spite of) the darkest times.

However—and this is a big *however*—an occasional side benefit, even a good opportunity for spiritual growth, does not make suffering right. When we try to justify suffering, find out the *why* of something, we not only exhaust ourselves in the pursuit of something that is not there, but put up an enormous roadblock on our road to healing. If my suffering produces strength, hope, and character, to use some of the biblical images, I may be blessed because of that. To say that those blessings justify the suffering or loss is to put our priorities backwards. It is like telling someone in the midst of suffering, "This is your cross to bear." It is also to say that somehow our needs or benefits are more significant than the life of someone we love.

Suffering comes. Injustice happens. God does not will it, cause it, or send it. Suffering also emerges because *grief hurts!* I can either spend what little energy I have left trying to justify or explain away bad things, or I can grab hold of the connection that enables me, however slowly, to move on to healing. The challenge and opportunity is to find God, to find connection, in the midst of suffering that is not right, is not purposeful, and can never be justified.

God is love. That is essential for me. God steps into my life in so many ways. I often do not know either the how or the why. Oftentimes my spirituality points out the reality of the connection, the blessing, long after the fact. Let's face it: In the middle of the war it is difficult to see the victories.

In the midst of grief we need to remember the "Parable of the Umbrella and the Extension Cord." Old habits linger, and they can become prominent when we are grasping at anything and everything (including umbrellas) as we journey through grief. As we struggle, however, we need to focus not on staying "dry," but on staying *connected*. There we will find our strength and even a hint of hope.

Soaking wet. That's how I feel! Tears upon tears. Grinding teeth as I hold back my anger. My gut tormented with the thrusts of guilt. It's all there, Lord. I am grieving. Now, when everything is overwhelming me, you tell me that I can grow in my love for you, that you will walk with me on this slippery, wet path to healing. I may throw my umbrella away, Lord, and even ponder throwing you *away. This is the time when everything is easily discarded.*

Help us to trust that you will never cast us aside. Amen.

Ouch!

The beeper had that special knack for finding me in the middle of the night. Of course, it never bothered on the restless nights when I was already half awake and needed to be doing something; it beeped when I was sleeping soundly!

The night I met Hazel (all names shared are fictitious) was one of those nights. I was sleeping soundly when the roar of the beeper seemed louder than the nearby freight trains. The message came from Oncology. "Please come and see Hazel. She is very upset and needs to talk."

My first thought was, "It's the middle of the night. Can't she talk to the nurse?" Duty called. Ministry awaited. Connections were sought. I dressed and went in to visit Hazel.

I had not met her before, but I knew from team rounds that she had been struggling with cancer for quite some time, mostly with radiation therapy, and this was her first inpatient treatment. While there was some success, it was limited at best, and the doctor was becoming more guarded.

I went in to meet Hazel. It was 3:00 a.m., yet all of the lights were on. There was no room for darkness in her room, at least what was visible. There was enough darkness surrounding her feelings. I introduced myself and grabbed a chair so I could listen more closely. Her first comment surprised me. "You're the grief man, aren't you?"

A question like hers is tough to field. Is it the real issue, or is she presenting a deeper issue, a turn in her feelings, a newly identified need, or an old story now coming to the surface? I indicated that I do a lot of listening, writing, and teaching about grief, but turned it back to her with, "Is there a reason why you are asking?"

She handed me a magic marker and said, "I want you to draw on my body the place where all the grief is, so that at my next treatment I can have the radiation therapist burn it out." That was quite a statement. It might have been easily dismissed by some, but remember that she was a woman with cancer who was used to having focal points drawn on her to help guide the radiation beam. Hazel was asking, If there is a cancer site, isn't there also a grief site?

I asked her, "Where do you think this grief place might be?" She talked about her head: all of the headaches from lack of sleep, from fear, from pain. She talked about how hard it was to read. Her eyes were blurred by medication and washed in tears. She pointed to her chest, "Where all of this stuff started." She pointed to her stomach, filled with nausea, and talked about how sick she was of seeing food commercials on television when she couldn't even handle ice chips. Her legs, growing weaker, were a particular worry to her because she liked to walk and jog. She looked at her hands, her ring finger bare because the swelling required that her wedding ring be cut off.

She located the grief, didn't she? It was from head to toe, and everywhere in between. Just as cancer filled more and more of her body, so did the tough feelings, the anguish, the fear, the desperation, and on some days (or maybe a few moments on some days), a hint of hope. She was feeling cancer all over because her feelings were all over her body. She didn't have to locate her grief, only to feel it.

Why did she raise these concerns with the chaplain? I knew the nurses on duty that night, and the two aides, and they were all very skilled listeners. They would have done a good job of giving Hazel permission to talk. They knew how to listen. Maybe it was because Hazel's pain had a strong spiritual element—her grief was physical, emotional, and spiritual. She was searching for clarity in her grieving. "Who am I? Why is this happening to me?" She was letting her God know that she hurt, and she was demanding (as well as begging) of God, "Be here with me."

A helpful tool for me in working with spirituality is to think in terms of four concentric circles—like the rippling effect of a stone dropped in a puddle that starts from the center and moves out. The four circles correspond to the following four key questions of assessment:

- How are you relating to your *self?*
- How are you relating to your *social network?*
- How are you relating to the *world around you?*
- How are you relating to *God?*

There are many theologians who will take exception to this formula. After all, we are supposed to be theocentric. We are to make God central in our lives. It is much like the Dean of Men at my college who, in his annual lecture to students on the "I Am Third" theme, would remind us that God comes first, everyone else is second, and, it would seem, the "I" in my life is a distant third.

Theologically speaking, God *is* at the center of my life. If it is any other way, my focus is distorted; it becomes a case of God (or god) emerging from me, rather than the other way around. Certainly in the Judeo-Christian tradition, God is not only central, but the one who reaches out to us. It is God the Initiator.

But my God is also a loving God. God has claimed me as a child, God's very own, loved and accepted where I am. God gives me bread not only to live, but to make the needed connections in my life. God talks with me, knows me by name, and carries me in arms of love. That is the kind of God-centered love that is at the heart of my spirituality and enables me to feel better about myself. It also demands of me that, as pastoral caregiver, I listen to another person's story, as it is central to his or her own life, and that I never move that person out of the centrality of his or her relationship with God.

Our relationship with God, our spirituality, often develops in the "ouches" of life. Church historian, theologian, and scholar Martin Marty recently addressed the subject of suffering on the *Chicago Sunday Evening Club*, a television show representing the local religious community. He led viewers through very careful waters of the "why" of suffering, to address the deeper issue, "Who am I in this suffering, and how will God and I go through this struggle together?"

Grief is spiritual because it is *mine*. Whatever disrupts my sense of worth, what life means to me, my sense of life's agenda or journey, is my story, and it is where I can meet God. Spirituality, like grief, is very personal. Every human being is spiritual, with a spirituality for his or her own need and journey.

If you were to put 250 people of the same denomination in one room, you would have a group with a lot of similarities, rituals, symbols, and actions that defined their commonality. That is religion (we will talk more about that later). In that same room are also 250 individuals with 250 spiritualities. Each is special.

Spirituality also hungers for community. Spirituality seeks markers and looks for reflectors to interpret life's meaning, life's experiences, so that we might understand where we are on that journey. By talking and listening to each other we move from isolation into community.

Spirituality is about community: "How am I relating to my spouse (or life without my spouse?), to family and friends?" These are spiritual concerns. To feel isolated from or abandoned by one's circle of friends ("They always seem to get upset because I cry, so now they just ignore me") is a spiritual crisis. To feel shut off from a caring religious community, either by a selected group of individuals, a religious leader, or an entire congregation, is a spiritual crisis. To find connection through a religious leader, a brother or sister in faith, or even through some passive participation in the rites of the religious community, is a spiritual blessing and an opportunity for growth in the midst of sorrow. To listen to a person's spiritual story is to listen to his or her need for community.

Why, Lord? I have questions and I demand answers. Answers will make me feel better—won't they? Then someone comes along and offers me an answer and the words sting and hurt all the more. There are no answers, but plenty of "ouches."

Comfort us, O Lord. Move us beyond answers and ouches to relationship and hugs. Amen.

Detours

Rites of spring: For those of us who live in the Chicago area, there are very specific spring rituals. Of course, there are the early blossoming flowers, the birds that sing, and the growth of all of the other things that make me sneeze. Joggers line the footpaths along the lake, while others pull into the various drives with their boats, hoping for early warmth that will give them permission to escape to the inviting seas. Stores have sales, people flock downtown to sightsee, and there is a bustle that says that winter is over.

Even sports have their rituals. Spring arrives and we look to the Chicago Bulls—well, actually, to Michael Jordan. Will he lead us to another championship? Meanwhile, across town, Cubs fans begin the annual debate, "How long 'til they are eliminated from the pennant race?"

No spring ritual affects Chicago quite like those feared, despised orange signs. "Construction Ahead." I know they afflict every city, and many a country path, but it always seems worse in Chicago. Every true Chicagoan knows that there are only *two* seasons, *winter* and *construction*! Newscasters struggle for new and creative ways to say the same old things. "Detours. Delays. Traffic ground to a halt."

Detours follow with the erection of more signs, the placement of more orange cones and barrels. They take us everywhere and nowhere. And, on some occasions, after we seem to have driven for hours, could it be that we have wound up back at the starting point?

Welcome to Chicago in the spring. And welcome to the world of grief. The bereaved know about detours firsthand. The whole journey itself is a detour, and with every passage into what seems like healing, comes another detour, another loss.

This chapter was placed here not to distract, but to offer a diversion or detour. It runs the risk of moving us away from our focus. That's always the risk. That's what detours do (or feel like), and they are as real in the world of the spiritual as they are in any other part of our journey. So let's take a little detour and talk about feelings and healing.

Feelings are where we experience grief, and feelings can assault our spiritual well-being. How often we cry out with the psalmist, "How long, O Lord?" Prayers (or the act of praying) just don't seem to grab us or no longer help us grab on to God. Worship brings only tears or we stare into space. The preacher talks a good story but she doesn't come and visit me. All of these folks talk about being the People of God, but do you think I can get one of them to sit down and just listen for awhile?

Spirituality is connection. We have said that. We also have said that the connection will get pulled, twisted, stepped on, stretched beyond recognition, just as we have been. Yet the connection remains, and when we move a little closer to our spiritual core, we have stepped another step toward healing.

It was a snowy Saturday afternoon, the skies were dark, and I was rushing about hoping that the beeper wouldn't squawk before I went off call. I had things to do, and I had to meet a friend and referee a basketball game.

No such luck. The beeper blared. "See Luther on 4-West" was the message that puzzled me. Luther was a dear, dear man with a measure of faith that was profound yet simple and trusting. We talked frequently and, while he was not doing well with his chemotherapy, he seldom would ask for anything, much less page for the chaplain. He knew we would talk each day and that seemed to meet his needs.

With the annoying sound of the beeper, I wondered what was wrong. Aware of time (only on call for another thirty minutes; meet my partner in forty-five minutes), I went to the hospital. Luther appeared tired, sitting up somewhat in his bed with the lights

26

dimmed. This was a clue, for usually Luther was the bright spot in my day and even the lighting would reflect his perpetual sense of hope. Not today.

As I entered the room, he murmured. I couldn't understand him. "Hello, Luther. I'm glad to see you, but I'm sorry I couldn't hear what you said." He looked up, winced as if in pain, and remarked, "How about those Hawkeyes?" To live in Iowa, as Luther did, meant to breathe the Hawkeye scent and spirit—and all of us became instant fans when we met Luther.

His team had indeed won an exciting football game, fighting back from a big deficit. But for this Luther had me paged? I was puzzled, cold, and a bit annoyed. Pressures of time and task can do that. I probably wasn't too subtle as I asked, "Luther, did you really page me in today to talk about the football game?" More pauses. More winces. He motioned. I sat beside him. He grabbed my hand. More waiting.

"Dick. Look at the mess the world is in: wars; three children were killed in a drive-by shooting; that sheriff's department across the river is under investigation. There are so many people dying of hunger, and look at all the food we grow, that I grow on my own farm. The national debt is growing. What a mess I'm leaving for my grandchildren." More pauses. More pain.

"Dick, with all of this, how could God possibly have time for me?" We finally cut to the heart of the matter, to the eternal struggle of our own relationship with God, and where faith and trust fit into the larger worldview. Luther felt insignificant.

The world *is* a very troubled place. Who *is* in charge of this spinning globe? To listen to a person's spiritual story is to enable that person to tackle these tough questions, questions that have less to do with answers and more to do with finding our way, and God's way, in a very complicated world.

Spirituality is not about fragmentation and it is not about little things. Spirituality is that which binds us to ourselves and keeps us accountable to our community, to the world around us, and to our God. All of that is important and all of that needs to be addressed, especially in a time of grief.

"What were my dreams? What is left to be done? Where am I going from here? How about those Hawkeyes! Does God have time for me?" Those were Luther's issues as he tried to find his way on his journey. They become our issues at times.

Spirituality is about healing. "The distinction between the physical and the spiritual is, I believe, false," wrote Wendell Berry in *Utne Reader* (September/October, 1995, p. 62). Just as disease strives to destroy, to break up community, to shatter wholeness into pieces, so does spirituality work to heal, to bring community, and to restore the fragments.

This spirituality is at the heart of the created order. Just as a sense of the Creator is the binding thread that is woven throughout the fabric of creation, so is spirituality the thread that binds creation to Creator, and Creator to creation. That is as true for the whole of creation as it is for each one of us.

It is such a bumpy ride, Lord. Detours. Potholes. New questions. More losses. With every acknowledgment of loss the pain rises to the top. Will I ever heal, Lord? Stay with me, God...please?! Amen.

Ultimates

What does life really mean? Does anything really matter when the most significant person in my life has died? I am supposed to "acknowledge the loss," say all the books, and with each new day my own awareness of loss increases. What or who can give meaning to that? I have unfinished business in my own life. There is no peace. Hope escapes me.

Those are not just words—they are at the heart of spirituality and the yearning of all who are bereaved. To listen to a bereaved person's story is to accept with love the tough and demanding words directed at God, at a religious community, at the deceased, or wherever the darts may fly. They are grief darts and they must fly freely.

If we are to assess the spirit of a person, we must stay with her and allow her to define, for herself, the ultimates in life. It is not our definition that matters. One social worker I spoke with was disheartened. Several of her clients were avowed atheists. "Haven't I failed them, allowing their loved ones to die without God?" She did not fail them. Her spiritual views may have given her a different agenda, but she stayed with the individuals. When we talked again some months later, she commented that the family members finally began to talk about their anger at God. They talked about the deep wounds caused by well-intended people who were always so busy trying to save them, or define their pathway to the Ultimate, that they never gave the clients a chance to speak or to search.

There are people who simply do not believe in God. Others have a deep trust in a personal God, but experience that Spirit in cultural ways far different from traditional Judeo-Christian expressions. Many Native American Indians have a profound sense of the spiritual, but realize their connection in symbols that seem foreign to, or have long since been forgotten or corrupted by, the dominant culture.

Some people may not talk about God. They still are searching for meaning. Some are burdened with guilt: a loved one suffers and they pray for a speedy and painless death, then are horrified by the meaning of those words. Where will they find forgiveness? Others are stuck in deep wounds, in the unfinished business of relationships that did not know wellness. Now, in their grief journey, they are not able to touch those feelings.

Hector was a sweet, older man, a recent widower. He came to the hospital with very serious cardiac problems. His family physician wrote orders for several consults. The first was to the chaplain.

Hector's heart was very diseased. It also was broken. His feelings were bogged down by the cultural and ethnic expectation that he be strong and proud (one of the detours that gets thrown at too many men). As he reminded me, "I must be strong for the children" (who happened to be fifty-eight, fifty-three, and fifty-two years old).

He lashed out at the God who "took" his wife first and left him here alone. The man was grieving. The man was facing possible death (though that didn't seem to matter to him at the moment) if he did not get immediate medical attention. God, hope, peace, understanding, and permission to grieve seemed so far away.

When I arrived, he assumed that the religious person was here to do some sacramental event with him or over him. He commented, "Isn't that nice. It isn't even a Catholic hospital and already a chaplain is here to see me." He then sat up, as if to say, "Okay, now *do* it." This wasn't about *doing*, however, it was about *being* with him. He needed permission to grasp what was already grabbing him.

I commented that his doctor asked me to stop by, and, yes, if there was a sacramental need I would see that it was met. I then sat by the bed and invited him to tell me his story. He talked about everything and everyone except his wife. The body language of one of his sons, who was in the room with Hector's other children, was saying, "Come on, Dad, he knows—talk about Mom." Sensing that the presence of his children made it hard for him to release, I invited them to visit the new waiting room where they would soon be spending some time. They seemed to understand and told Dad they would be back in a few minutes. They winked at me and also looked very relieved as they quickly and quietly left the room.

We went back to the story and to his heart history. I asked him when his heart problems started. He commented, "Boy, I really began to notice it a few months ago. It felt so heavy. I walked around with heavy weights pounding into my chest and pulling me down." He breathed aloud, more tears, only now he allowed them to flow. "It was April 17th."

"April 17th?"

"Yes, the day my Rose died." He cried. He paused. He smiled. Out came the story. "It all started that day—*and it all ended that day.*" He grabbed for my hand. "I lost my Rose that day and I lost my life that day. Nothing mattered. The chest pains worsened. Who cared? I certainly didn't.

"Damn it! Why did she go and die? What kind of a husband am I that I would let her die first? I should have taken better care of her. I don't care that the suffering from cancer stopped. If one more person told me to feel good that her suffering was over, I would have…"

He sobbed, he yelled, he tossed and turned. He was hooked to a monitor and I could see the lines going every which way. His nurse checked in. She came by the bedside, patted him gently (giving him permission to go on with his story), listened quietly, then left him to talk with me.

Hector talked about their wedding, the special priest friend who did the wedding and then baptized the children. He mentioned every child by name, explaining why Rose picked that particular name. He spoke of his guilt at not being a better husband, lover, and provider. His feelings slipped into hopelessness, as well as the helplessness that landed him in this place.

Ethical dilemmas, truly a spiritual fact for many, came up. "The doctor kept pushing. 'More drugs,' she would say, or 'Let's just keep going. I don't think this is the time to be stopping.' I kept hearing the doctor's words, but Rose kept saying, 'Hector, it will be just fine. It is time to let me go.'" He was shaking. "Let her go? No way. More treatment. I failed her. Will God forgive me? Will Rose forgive me?"

In Rose's facing of the Ultimate in her life, Hector was thrust into a whole new world. Everything in his life, his relationship, his ability to find forgiveness, meaning, hope, ethics, trust of the medical system, self-respect, justice, God (there's a personal checklist for you when exploring a person's spirituality) had been torn apart by Rose's death. His cultural filters prevented him from pouring out his story and it all landed on his diseased heart.

There is no surgery for broken hearts, but there is healing. It began in that conversation as Hector touched his pain, halted his running, and—in the embrace of the God whose presence was symbolized by the presence of the chaplain—faced Rose's Ultimates, and his own, in a new and healing way.

Was God present for him? As I was getting ready to leave, Hector smiled broadly. "Hey chaplain, I thought you came here to anoint me." I smiled. Before I could tell him that I would call his priest, he said, "Don't worry. God already did."

In all of the endless telephone commercials we suffer through these days, the old slogan that once was commonplace has been noticeably absent: "Reach out and touch someone." That is the eternal challenge, initiative, and hope in our spiritual journey. For me, there is no eternity apart from the endless love of God that I am privileged to experience as God's child day after day. It is God's love for me in Jesus that sustains me. That is ahead, whether that *ahead* is the next few minutes of this day, a lifetime—however long that may be—or forever. Others have a different concept of time and eternity. Here it is, the human drive to reach beyond ourselves to something—for me, Someone—that is beyond all of this. Here is my hope and here is life's meaning.

Hector found comfort in the eternal promises in which he trusted for his wife and, one day, for himself. His all-consuming grief had blinded him, denied him access to the hope in those promises. Through grieving, he was no longer ignoring his spiritual journey. In that attentiveness, he claimed the connection that was always there and he moved closer to his experience of healing and hope.

I have a story, Lord. It is about loss, but the plot is about love. Help me to affirm and respect my story. Guide me through it. Help me to listen to myself in an affirming way. By the way, God—are you listening? Amen.

Lost

The other night I had an early evening appointment on the north side of Chicago. It was a good reason to clear the schedule afterward and play. Chicago invites that. Off to the city I went. I found a parking garage just a short walk from Water Tower Place. Everything was just right.

The car was parked, the weather was beautiful, and off I walked. I even remembered to mark the garage ticket with the location of the car. I went to three bookstores. I got two new books and four newspapers from England. Then I went to a new restaurant for a quiet dinner: Outstanding.

It was a delightful time, until I had to find my car. I had the ticket in my hand, and I knew exactly where I was going. Ha! I walked and walked. I even went to the correct intersection. Not only was there no car, but there was no parking garage! I was losing my mind—the *crazies*. If I asked people for help, they backed away. I had a suit on, and showed the parking ticket, and still they backed away—I was crazy and *contagious*. How could I explain to people my predicament when they cast me aside as a leper?

There were no markers. I could have been in a desert, for all the help the street signs were. No one told me that Delaware Place and Delaware Street were not the same. No one made it clear that buildings on a corner do not always have the address of the street where the front door faces. I was losing it. I was lost.

Grief is a lot like being lost. The markers we have relied on—family, friends, God, ourselves—all seem to change. No one is there to point the way. There are no signs.

What do we do when God seems lost? God is the one who is supposed to find us. Isn't God the shepherd, the one who "carries us in the palm of his hand?" When I am lost, I want to be found—sometimes. At other times, I feel like saying, "Leave me alone; I'll do this myself." Walls go up. Walls come down.

We are so blinded by the reality of our loss that it distorts everything we see, feel, or experience. Grief is a filter, and everything in our life, at least for now, goes through that filter until we are ready to release the filter. A loving, caring God understands and respects our feelings because God understands and respects grief.

I found my car by demanding that the markers work for me. I had the address on the ticket, and remembered that *east* and *west* meant something. I knew to watch for the large green signs that designate a city lot. I stayed with it, also tuning in to some other markers—a restaurant, a church, a park—things that had always been there but that the blinders had kept me from acknowledging. I found the garage. I took no chances with stairs, but walked right up the ramp that my car had traveled until I experienced the grand reunion.

When grief comes, our relationship with God may not feel the same anymore. The change may seem permanent, or it may depend on the direction of our anger and guilt that day. The religion in our life may heap more frustration than faith on the situation. It isn't easy to be or feel lost.

Like the parable of the lost sheep, my spirituality connects me to a God who is always connected to me, always seeking me (whether I am seeking him or not). So I can go back to the signs: for the lost car, the signs that designate city parking lots; in my faith journey, experiencing (or enduring) another sermon, spending time with Scripture, prayers that seem to be going nowhere (sometimes they are the most powerful ones), the sacraments, reading a devotional book, sitting through at least part of a worship service. As we seek connection with God, we experience the sense of being found and embraced. It is when we are most lost that God is most found.

A light went on in my heart today. It dawned on me that there is love, there is hope. Am I starting to heal? Am I starting to move from remembering a death to remembering a life? Have I stepped, at least a foot at a time, out of the lost column into the found? Amen.

Thirst

I find these days that my spiritual self is growing. The last few months have been rich in many ways, but on some days it is all overshadowed by dark clouds of sorrow and loss. I have battled with the death of my mother, the serious health problems of another loved one, struggles within my church (or at least its hierarchy), and all the adjustments of a professional transition. Through it all—despite it and because of it—my spiritual connections have been strengthened. Despite deep resentment, flaring episodes of bitterness, struggles with guilt and shame, and all of the other standard symptoms associated with spiritual wilderness, my spiritual connection grew. Faith has meant more. Prayer has meant more. The Lord's Supper has meant more. The great hymns of the church and my access to music, have meant more—*spirituality*.

The *religion* suffers, however. I find myself distancing from hierarchy, bureaucracy, religious expectations, congregational interaction. This will heal, hopefully, but I find that I must distance myself from issues and individuals causing me pain, who violate my boundaries, and who threaten to cloud my spiritual horizon.

Religion. Within it are some very caring bureaucrats, wonderfully forgiving and understanding communities, and very good people who offer not judgment but hope, not words but Word, not distance but embrace.

It would be easy to say, "Spirituality is good" or "Religion is bad." Some of my readers would be delighted if I would finally render an opinion on that one. After all, it would clear up so much confusion (or so we think). Besides, it would validate all of my wounds, grudges, hurts, and wrong opinions about religion, a congregation, a specific minister.

Some of us have been deeply hurt by a church, by an abusive religious leader, by callous congregational members. That does not make religion bad, any more than it is valid to say that spirituality is inherently good. That is not always guaranteed. I have worked with many victims of abusive and addictive spiritualities.

No, it's not about good or bad but about *difference.* Spirituality and religion *are not the same thing.* Believe me when I say that no words on a page can simplify all of this. Contemporary society mixes the words freely—says one when it means the other and often dilutes both words in order to give them new meaning.

It isn't easy to discern the difference between spirituality and religion. Battles with the church are complicated and very personal. They also are valid. Woven through it all is the question, "Why isn't God doing something with all of this?" Or the question that has plagued our hearts for the whole history of humankind, "Where is God in my suffering?"

The beeper goes off and I go to the unit down the hall. The nurse, herself struggling with religious problems, delights to tell me that, in essence, the religious community screwed up, and somehow the chaplain was either responsible for the problem or for finding the right solution. Her message? "Mrs. Levi in Bed 2 is very angry that her rabbi has not been in to visit with her."

That issue is common for rabbis, ministers, priests, and all other religious leaders, ordained or not. Often it's a computer problem. A person either did not give a religious preference when admitted or the clerk didn't ask. A name is omitted from the list. In the midst of the crisis, no one in the family bothered to call the minister—or even had time to. Some clergy feel they are too busy to make calls or just leave it to the chaplain. It isn't always easy to correct this problem, which causes much hardship and lots of blame. It is a religious problem.

Or was it a religious problem for Mrs. Levi? Did she simply want to talk with her rabbi? Did she want someone to read to her from the Torah, or to check that the dietitian really understood what she meant by a kosher diet? It's not always easy to understand what people are searching for. Mrs. Levi knew her rabbi was only stationed part-time at her synagogue and would be in town in a few days. Maybe it was just the reassurance of knowing that he knew she was in the hospital and was praying for her. Maybe that's all she was asking. Maybe she was asking a whole lot more.

I sat with Mrs. Levi. She talked first about her rabbi, then reminded me that I needed to inform the dietary department about all of the different dimensions of kosher meals. When we had worked through all the business at hand, she sighed, looked reflective, and then cried, "God was there for Abraham and Sarah. God was all over the psalms. God spoke through the prophets. Why can't I find God here, in Bed 2?"

Did Mr. Frank, another patient, really want a lecture on the theology of the sacraments? Did he have some magical belief that if he had Communion every day, everything would be okay? Maybe he was searching for a whole lot more. Could it be that questions that seemed to deal with admissions records and parish documentation, statements that seemed more concerned about sacramental scheduling, had a spiritual base?

"My priest comes as often as he can," said Mr. Frank. "The eucharistic ministers come every Sunday morning. Chaplain, do you know how wonderful it feels every day, usually before my first medications, breakfast, and those endless tests, to hear, to taste, 'This is the Body of Christ?'" Yet the staff was noting in the chart, "Mr. Frank seems more depressed. The medication is working, the tumor is shrinking, yet he seems to doubt it all." The message was the same at interdisciplinary rounds, and the doctor noted it in orders for visits both from the chaplain and from the psychologist.

After we conversed a while, Mr. Frank revealed that he had been abused as a child. When he tried to report it, he was chastised: "How dare you say such horrible things!" The patient experienced those harsh words as, "Shame on you. It's your fault. You are a bad person." Now he was a victim of abuse for a second time. It wasn't at the hands of a loved one, but at the hands of a disease. It was the old tape: "Shame on you. It's your fault. You are a bad little boy." He was seventy-six years old, reliving tapes that were now sixty-nine years old.

This was about old messages, rooted in his spiritual journey, that required special care. To Mr. Frank, the guilt and shame were very real, and he needed to release them through a forgiveness that would restore him to wholeness. The daily sacrament helped him do that.

Through a discussion of his spirituality and his religion, we finally were able to touch the pain of those wounds. His priest also shared in the story and the healing. Anointing was a whole new experience. Bread and wine were Body and Blood as they had always been for him, but now with so much more peace. He realized that he was not the cause of his cancer. It wasn't about cause but about disease. What originally appeared to be a religious problem was actually a problem of emotional baggage that was healed through his spirituality and his religion.

Spirituality and religion are not the same. Spirituality is "I"; it is how I personally journey with my spirit, how I relate to God, and the active embrace of God in my life. Religion is "We," where I find community, where I seek out the resources, comfort, and insights of people with similar understandings and awareness. Religion is where we become a family (congregation) of believers—praising, studying, being nourished, then scattering for service as a religious community of spiritual beings.

Spirituality and religion serve different purposes. This became apparent to me a few years ago when grocery stores became depots for bulk purchases. Do you remember the big barrels and boxes with a serving spoon or scoop attached to a long cord (never a long enough cord, if you ask me)? First it was bulk cookies and dog biscuits. Then candy, detergent, and many other products. We told ourselves (because the signs said so, and we wanted to believe it) that it was cheaper this way. We were avoiding the cost of the fancy packaging, probably helping the environment, and also were able to choose the quantity that we wanted.

I still needed a container. If I were merely to stick my hand into the powdered detergent, I could grab some product—maybe even enough for a load of wash. I could clench my fist and possibly accomplish the impossible task of getting all of it through the checkout line, to the car, across town, out of the garage (don't forget the other groceries), through the back door which I have to unlock (try doing that with one hand!), and into the washer. I wonder how much detergent would be left?

The package is necessary, important, valuable. It isn't the final product, of course. That's the detergent. Because of the packaging, however, I have better access to that product when it's needed, I am able to direct it to the right place for the appropriate use, and I still have access to it in the future.

Religion is the packaging; spirituality is the product. When I stop during a presentation for a glass of water, I am glad to have the glass there. I would waste a good deal of time trying to find a water fountain (they're never handy), or would look very foolish trying to carry water in my hand from the pitcher in the back of the room to the podium. The glass is important—it provides a place for the connection to the water—*but it is the water that quenches my thirst.* My religion is the glass; my spirituality is the water—hopefully not conflictual, just different.

Religion is like family. It experiences the same struggles, imperfections, and diversity as any family. Still, it can be community—a family of wounded folks sharing different needs, stories, and wounds; but still family, still embracing, still caring. It is also in religion that we can find the rituals we need to interpret our faith, explore our grief, and find the connection we need to embrace our sorrow as we move toward healing.

A bereaved parent and friend spoke of special prayers she prayed daily in the temple that were such a hope and comfort for her. Some days she didn't even hear the words. Other days she didn't remember going to the temple. Christian friends, Jewish friends, nonaffiliated friends joined her. The ritual of habit surrounded her when she needed it most. When she was ready to move on, the visits to temple for that ritual lessened. Soon new things took over. The spirit grew. She healed, moment by moment, prayer by prayer.

Some old rituals will be cast aside. A loving community of

believers will adjust when they share a common focus as a bereaved community. Some rituals will become heightened in their importance or reshaped for a new appearance and a new presence in the lives of the participants. Some entirely new rituals will step in to fill the void (if congregation members are open to that), some staying around for just a short while, others assuming a whole new place for the community of believers.

I was asked to prepare the Sunday morning closing-day liturgy for this year's annual conference of The National Catholic Ministry to the Bereaved. This community ritual, although only fifteen minutes, promised an opportunity to bring closure on all that had been shared and learned and to open a door to new possibilities as the people departed for home and work.

The image of the butterfly came to mind—a universal symbol for life and hope, used by Roman Catholics, Protestants, Jews, and those of no particular faith expression. Hope beyond hopelessness, life beyond death, beginnings emerging despite endings.

Time-honored rituals were valuable at that time for the group: a reading, a prayer, a visual sign, music. After a reading about butterflies, Brother Michael McGrath sat down with a handful of marking pens and created a poster-sized butterfly. A litany was created around the colors in the wings, one color for each feeling common to the grief experience, followed by a hopeful word of Jesus from his ministry—verses and responses as the community shared. It was a community using all the resources at its disposal to gather around the Easter message of resurrection that is at the heart of the community's story.

Sister Mauryeen O'Brien had school children cut out and color 200 small butterflies. What a sight! Each one was different, a helpful reminder that each of us is unique, as are our stories and journeys. And yet we are bound together in a commonality that transcends difference, creating a celebration of diversity.

Each person was given a butterfly and a pencil. On the back of the butterfly, people were invited to list one or more deceased. They were then invited to remember these deceased in prayer. Next they were invited to entrust these concerns to the larger community. All of the butterflies were gathered in a common basket and brought to the Mass. There, at the table, with bread and wine, Body and Blood, all of the loved ones were remembered and lifted to God in prayer. Ritual, community—all were gathered together and then allowed to scatter as refreshed, blessed people.

Was it an effective ritual? For others, I cannot say, though I did receive some good feedback. It meant a great deal to me—and I wasn't even there. I was called home the day before because my mother had died. I entrusted the ritual to the larger community and flew home to a new agenda, a new loss, and a need to find rituals that would lead me through this new detour in my wilderness journey. The ritual of that particular community sustained me, because I knew that my mother was named on several of those butterflies and placed on the altar for God's tender care. A Roman Catholic organization remembered in their prayers, with their rituals, a Congregationalist woman who died and her Lutheran son.

Rituals do not exist for themselves, nor to stop or end the suffering. And just because they have been there doesn't make them right, *but it does make them available*. Rituals serve the group. As Rabbi Earl Grollman said so well recently in a lecture, "Ritual becomes important to us when we give it meaning *for ourselves*, at this moment in our lives." If it has purpose *today*, then grab it today. Let all of the traditions and rituals of your religion be potential gifts for you, and, when necessary, demand your right to make new rituals. Remember, *it is your journey, and yours alone*.

Water, water everywhere. I thirst for so much, or maybe just a little bit. People offer gallons of the popular beverages, and I can't find an ice chip to quench the burning in my soul. God, you are the water that quenches my every thirst. Help me to "Taste and see that the Lord is good." Amen.

Listen

Parables are a wonderful way of identifying and sharing a story. The Christian Scriptures are rich with examples of Jesus teaching through the stuff of parables: rocks, soil, trees, seeds. Such things were the common images and language of his day, and Jesus used them to his advantage in telling the story of his ministry.

What follows isn't just a nice exercise for the bereaved who happen to go to a church or synagogue or profess some specific belief in God. This exercise is for all of us, ordinary people thrust into extraordinary situations (a good definition for loss) and trying to find meaning, direction, and hope. We question—those endless "why" questions. We find our old ways of believing and trusting challenged, tested, and possibly discarded. We may discover that the treasures of our faith have grown immensely and we have grown, too. This is common in grief.

What is also common in grief is the inability of those on the journey, and even the "experts" who surround them, to test the spiritual waters, to stay with the tough words and impossible questions.

The worksheet presented on page 43 is a valuable tool for individual therapy, individual study, group work (such as with an entire family), and teaching. The format began a few years ago with a chart developed by my good friend, Dr. Patrick DelZoppo. It has been expanded to a multi-tiered approach, enabling the person to claim his or her spirituality and religion (and, in some cases, to define it), and then trace these dynamics from the time before the loss, during the height of the grief experience, and now.

Many people identify tremendous concern about God or their religious community. It is often hard to discern if this is a legitimate consequence of poor care during the bereavement journey, or just a heightened expression of what spirituality and/or religion meant to that person before the loss. Others use the same chart to diagram a definite pattern of growth from previous expressions of faith and understandings of spiritual community.

The value of this exercise is that it may represent the first time that an individual can finally clarify needs, what he or she is searching for, what is helping on the faith journey, and what (or who) may be standing in the way.

Work with a pencil and a big eraser. We are not looking for neatness, correct dogma, all of the right theological words, or liturgical art or symbols. We are providing a tool that is as fluid as your grief journey and spiritual walk. We are trying to provide you with some handles, something to hold on to in this madness, and, hopefully, the reassurance that Someone is holding on to you as you are grieving.

At the top in the section marked "A," you are invited to identify your understanding of spirituality and religion. Some of the earlier chapters in this book may provide some resources and definitions for you. Let your heart and faith be your guide. Sentences are okay, but so are words, a collection of words in no particular order, a diagram, or a picture. It is your story, so make it work for you. Some people draw a horizontal line through the middle of each box, creating two boxes. You can then identify definitions as you experience them now, and in the lower tier, as you would like them to be.

In the section labeled "B," you track (and treasure) your experiences, feelings, and beliefs about spirituality and religion as they were before the loss, at the height of your grief experience, and now. Focus on yourself, your story, your relationships. Don't try to write what you feel others believe or expect you to believe. This is not about pleasing God, the other people in your life, or even yourself. It's about understanding: simply figuring out where you are, what's working for you, and what's a trouble spot. It's about shaking it all up, tossing it out on the table, and grabbing hold for the next step in your emotional, social, and spiritual journey.

Claim your story, even the dark corners or blind spots. You don't need to have everything right or worked out. You just need to identify the inner resources that are already there, or claim new ones, for your journey to healing.

Maybe there are some parts of the story that are stumbling blocks. Maybe you are waiting for me to explore some feelings I can't or won't get to. Maybe you are waiting for me to let go. Thank you for valuing my story. Help me to listen more closely to my inner story. Thank you, too, for listening. Amen.

A

"I"	"We"
My definition of spirituality	My definition of religion

B

My experiences, feelings, and beliefs

Before the loss	During the crisis	Where am I now?

Blame

"What kind of God would allow a thing like this to happen to me?" It is a question I have been asked almost as many times as I have asked it. A man slips on a banana peel in a bar, falls, spills his drink, and protests the injustice of this accident.

Why did God let this happen?

Why was the banana peel there?

Why didn't God catch me (or at least my drink) before I fell?

Why did my baby die?

Why is there cancer?

Why did that drunk driver plow into my car?

Why now?

We want someone or Someone to be responsible. It seems to fit better when someone is in charge, someone is responsible, and someone can be blamed. Well-intended religious folk don't help. Yes, they are struggling to find the resources of faith in this impossible situation, as you are also searching. But "It's God's will," or "God only gives you what you can handle," or "The Lord gives and the Lord takes away" are of little help to me and, frankly, very hurtful.

It's normal to seek some explanation. We hurt. We are scared. We are angry. We are doubting. Life isn't worth living for us anymore, and we want some way or Someone to help us get through this. We think that if somehow we can make sense out of this loss, that will make things right and we will feel better. Yet it is impossible, and for good reason. Loss isn't healed by making it right. Knowing everyone is mortal, that sometimes death appears to be a better option than a life of suffering, does not make any of this right. It isn't right, because it isn't about right and wrong.

Trying to make it right occupies our time for a while. It's even a healthy form of denial. But it is not a fix. We are not talking about breaking and fixing, a quick mend like a tear in fabric. The fabric is beyond mending. It is gone. A new cloth must be sought, one that can only emerge through the rugged redesigning of who we are as we move toward something we will eventually experience as healing.

Still, it seems easy to blame God because God is greater than we are. Doesn't that make God responsible for everything? If I blame God, I am also taking myself off the hook. I don't have to look at my flaws, my hurts, or my personal challenges. If everything is in God's control, I can just give it over to God.

But who wants to trust in a God who caused my loved one to die? We simply can't understand why tragedy happens. But we can feel—and we can heal. We do not find healing in answers, blame, or justice, but in the connection that binds us to ourselves, to the ones we love, and to our God.

At the heart of grief is not loss but love. It is the love which makes all of this so important, and it is the love we are working for. It is the love we want to cherish and claim, a love that enables us to move to memories of the one who lived and still lives in us. Isn't that more comforting than being stuck in the rut of blame?

Lord, the screen on my spiritual computer has gone blank. My account is overdrawn, my vision fogged, and all the roads seem blocked. I want to blame you, myself, maybe even my loved one who died. After all, isn't someone supposed to be at fault here?

I feel so angry at times; at other times, hurt, alone, or just plain scared. Help me to know that you stand by me in those tough, low moments, even when I may be pushing you away. Help me to trust that the more I push you away, the tighter you will hold me with your love. Amen.

Strength

Reverend Will B. Dunn is one of my favorite cartoon characters. What a rascal! Some would say that he represents all that is wrong with established religion. That may be true. But maybe he is also a helpful friend as we attack the things we feel like attacking. Maybe there is a gift in his madness that brings us to the heart of the matter.

He is current with every trendy aspect of the church, this preacher. He has an Automatic Teller Machine that takes deposits only. He probably accepts offerings by credit card, too. For some, this smacks of all that is wrong with religion. "Take, take, take." It's easy to think of the church as being around just to take our money: "Where two or three are gathered in my name, there shalt an offering be taken." Bingo every Friday night. Let's sell these candy bars or raise funds for this project. Budget. Stewardship.

For some, church is all about "taking." Maybe that has been your own experience. When I listen to people report their experiences, it's no wonder that they have such a disastrous view of religion. I had one counselee take notes on his minister's sermons. For three weeks the sermons averaged twenty-seven minutes in length, and over sixty percent of each message was about "what you must give to the church."

For others the issue is entitlement. For example, I have been baptized, confirmed, ordained; I have all of this theological training, plus additional clinical training for chaplaincy and bereavement work—I even have the papers to prove it. Doesn't that entitle me to something out of the church, or out of God?

Listen to the very profound promises God has made to us:

The Lord is my shepherd, I shalt not want. (Psalm 23:1)
I am with you always. (Matthew 28:20)
I know my own and my own know me. (John 10:14)
He will feed his flock like a shepherd; he will gather the lambs in his arms, and carry them in his bosom. (Isaiah 40:11)
Come to me, all you that are weary and are carrying heavy burdens, and I will give you rest. (Matthew 11:28)

You get the picture. If we have come to know a loving, caring God who has promised to love us, guard us, and guide us, then death—even death that is expected—threatens that promise. When conditions surrounding the loss expand our level of pain, horror, or suffering, the promise shrinks even more. It may come to a point where not only have we lost a loved one, but we have lost God—or at least the God we believe can possibly make a difference in our lives.

Life is not about deposits and credits, but withdrawals. Does God have something to offer us now? How do I pray to God to watch over my children when one child died? (Maybe I will even say, "when God allowed one child to die.")

These are tough theological struggles, and too many searching folk are shoved away by ministers who refuse to listen, who "correct" them for faulty theology, or who recite "all the right answers"—without having a clue about what this particular person is asking or longing for.

We are trying to connect. We are trying to find the symbols of our faith to hold us up, calm us down, quench our thirsts, and feed our hungers. Okay, we're not going to make sense out of all or any of this, but at least we need to find some reason to go on with our own life journey.

Old or new understandings, old or new approaches to spirituality—it probably doesn't matter. What does matter is that we find strength from that which is neither old nor new, but timeless.

Help me, God, to find the strength that stays with us in all of our questions, all of our explosive feelings, all of our arguments, excuses, and doubts.

Stay with me, and be my strength. Amen.

Found

In Great Britain they do not have a "lost and found," but a place for "found property." It does seem more positive. Things do get found—forgotten umbrellas, missing glasses. Maybe even a wallet. It is nice when things are found.

But things still do get lost, and sometimes *we* are what's lost. We bang into roadblocks, crash into walls, slip on slick surfaces. What's worse, we are often convinced that God has done the same thing.

Look at the headlines. How many reminders do we need until

we realize that no one is really in charge here? If that is the case, what hope is there, and what chance is there for us to heal? Take the child who, wanting to have urgent attention for his prayer, asks if God has a fax number. We know where God is, but we wonder if God has a fax number, so that we can get instant access and even faster answers.

What *do* we have to do to get God's attention? Maybe we have tried everything and all we come up with is wrong numbers. Maybe God has an unlisted number. Sometimes it's so hard to connect with anyone, including God. Sometimes we look for meaning and hope in all the wrong places. No answers. Maybe not even a lot of strength at the moment. Maybe only a hint of direction.

Lord, help me just to find enough strength to take a first step. And, oh, yes, please point me in the right direction! Amen.

Past

Now be honest, those of you who are parents. How many of you, around Christmas, have said at least once, "Now you better be good—remember, Santa Claus is watching"? It's a wonder any child ever survived Santa Claus or Christmas, or discovered the true meaning of the holiday spirit of giving.

When we try to discipline through manipulation, we often end up with empty promises and even emptier symbols. What kind of a relationship do we have with a God of love if the only God we know is one who is constantly spying on us, as if salvation were based on whether we are naughty or nice? Salvation, like love, is a gift.

Cathy MacDougall is well into her eighties. She was my Sunday School teacher in the third grade. She taught me very wise lessons way back then, and she still teaches me when I wander back to my home congregation on Staten Island.

I was way up in the choir loft working on an improvisation

48

based on my mother's favorite hymn, "Rock of Ages." It was to be my offering to God, in loving memory of my mother, at her funeral. I saw Cathy at her busiest, the Altar Guild lady, making sure everything was just right for the service. I yelled down a greeting. Cathy's eyes are failing. She walked through the church to see who this was. Once she recognized me, she shouted up a warm and loving greeting with a big smile.

She said, "Now Dick, we know Mom is happy now, at peace and with your Dad. She really believed in God. I just know everything is okay. I also know it isn't okay with you. You are hurting now. It will take time, but give it that time. Jesus will help you." I was eight years old for those first lessons, and fifty for this lesson, but both times she embraced me—not with threats, not with judgment, but with love.

That has been the message about God that I have heard throughout my life. Many people have not. Many know a "god" of regimentation, expectations, rules and regulations: Do not drink. Do tithe. Do this. Don't do that.

That isn't a loving God. That isn't even God. That is religious abuse which leaves us crying out, "Oh no, not Santa Claus *and* God." If we know only a judgmental, get-even God who is spying on us, I doubt we will find any peace and healing, at least any that encourages our spiritual connection.

God is not about manipulation but about a relationship built on love and trust from which then comes responsible service. People, even well-intended people, place those other ideas on us. If that is where you are, that is your right (I will pray for you), *but don't put it on me.*

And then there's the phrase "God's will." This is something that has been more misunderstood and has done more damage in bereavement caregiving than any other catch phrase, with the possible exception of "I know how you feel." Who are we to presume to know God's will? We don't. We may believe that God wants what is good and healthy for us spiritually, and Scripture supports that, but that is a far cry from some pronouncement of a minister, relative, friend, or passerby trying to give meaning to that which has no meaning for us.

A year ago I saw this obituary:

49

Thank you, God. Thank you, Jesus. Our little Danny is safely in your arms. He is the boy soprano in your choir of angels, the rose in your flower garden, the smile on your horizon of love.

It really troubled me, not only because a child died, but because of the words themselves. They represented all the worst I could imagine about a coerced or manipulated faith. The obituary identified Danny as a lad who died at the age of three days, and then followed with details about funeral arrangements.

My first thought was to "set them straight on their theology." See, I meant well, and I have very good credentials in theology and pastoral care. Doesn't that give me the right? I resisted the temptation to lecture them. Instead, I put together a packet of materials on grief for parents who have experienced the death of a young child, including some carefully selected materials on faith and grief, and sent them off with a personal note. I did not know these people. They did not come through the hospital I was serving at the time. I shared with them that I am a bereaved parent and a grief counselor, and would be happy to visit with them at any time.

Several months later I was speaking at a diocesan conference about grief and spirituality. There were many questions. After the people left and I was quietly gathering my things, I noticed a young couple still sitting in the back of the room. I figured they were waiting for someone, so I continued my packing. Not paying attention, I looked up to see them standing right by me. I introduced myself. They were very pleasant and shared their names, although I made no connection to that obituary.

"Dick, you were so kind to send us that wonderful note and the grief materials. They were very helpful." I was still trying to make the connection, because I send many cards and a lot of material through the mail. "Our little Danny died from congenital heart defects. It all was so hard. We thought it was our fault, because we both have a medical history of heart disease in the family. Everyone was telling us what to do, how to behave, and what to believe. All we wanted was what any parents would want for their child, to know that he or she is safe, receiving good care, and happy.

"Since we wouldn't have the chance to give that to Danny— but, oh, how we wanted the chance to try—we were going to make sure that Danny was okay. Our obituary was going to make sure. We were telling Danny, ourselves, all of our friends and relatives, and God just the way it had to be. Danny had to be fine. We could not handle any more failure."

We sat and visited for a long time. We talked about guilt, fear, hopelessness—about all the things that bereaved parents feel. We talked about faith, about things that helped and things that hurt. It was getting late and we picked a time when we could visit again. They closed with these words, "Thanks, Dick, for at least not telling us that our obituary was wrong, that our words were wrong, or, like some of the family, that this was absolutely the way it had to be. We were so confused and so lost. We just needed time to sort things out, and for someone to listen."

If you know only a judgmental God, a God whose "will" requires that terrible things happen, that is the God you will know in your grieving. It doesn't have to be that way. If those who surround you know some version of that same God, they do not have the right to place that on you.

Where is God in your life? What is your inner strength? Do you have the freedom and opportunity to reach for those inner resources?

Spare me, Lord, from hurtful words, judgmental friends, and even those friends and caregivers who love me and mean well, but who just don't understand. Please give me the strength and the insight not to "fix them," but to find where I need to be, and where you will be with me. Amen.

Trust

"Lord, teach us to pray."

The ministry I founded, called CONNECTIONS - SPIRITUAL LINKS, is about helping people find connections to God, to purpose, to hope, and to a reason to experience life again. Much of this ministry is in correspondence with folks who write letters, usually after hearing a lecture or presentation.

There are always questions. Some come during or right after a presentation; others, months later. Some letters are just a few words. One was eighteen pages, legal size, handwritten on both sides. Most of them come to the point of asking, "Teach me how to pray."

All of them have expressed not just a desire for help with prayer, but the bold and tearful statement, "I am not sure I can ever pray again." Some make it even more specific: "Why should I pray? It doesn't really matter, anyway. "I prayed, and I prayed…

> …yet my son did not make it home safely. The drunk driver did a better job than God."

> …for 'healing,' and yet the cancer kept spreading."

> …She's so young, with children to raise. Why?"

> …but he lingered and lingered. He always believed in a loving, powerful God. He withered away to nothing. How could I trust a God that took so long to 'bring him home'?"

> …for a healthy baby, and look what I got."

"I prayed, and I prayed…" We trust. We believe. We pray. Hearts are broken. Doubts grow. Others seem to laugh at us when we still want to believe that God loves us, that God makes a difference, and that God still really cares.

Of course, there are those around us who can explain all of our questions, longings, and doubts: "It was his time." "God had better plans in mind." "You just needed to believe more." "Now, now…good things always come out of suffering."

Trust in God often is defeated more by the people who seem determined to help God out, than by God. Job had lots of advice offered to him. Jesus cried out on a cross and was jeered while others gambled away his possessions. We pray for peace, and there is an increase in gun sales. We commit to the Bread of Life, and more and more people die from starvation in a world that has food but can't overcome transportation problems, financial agendas, and political barriers. And we are supposed to trust? Why would anyone even ask about prayer? But they do. "Teach me to pray."

There it is. Connection. Relationship. We need help. We see

the walls of certainty and hope cracking all around us. The hammer of grief's despair continues to pound into us. We cry out, "How long, O Lord?" and we wonder if anyone is listening. We often are so lost in our grief, so consumed by our anger, doubt, guilt, and fear (all of which are often compounded by the religious community or religious beliefs that filter many of our grief experiences) that all we can do is fold our hands and surrender.

Look at the hands: trusting, searching, hoping, despairing. They are closed. It is impossible to get within them. It's like when you play the game, "Guess which hand." Something is hidden, and the one looking for the candy or other object is desperate to get inside. But the fist is tight, the grasp is rigid, and nothing moves in or out. It's often the same with our prayer life, our faith, our longing.

Anyone who tells me that they have true faith, and never a doubt, is either foolish or dead. It means that they believe everything is fine, all worked out, and in its proper place. I suspect they are on a very pointed peak, with a deep valley awaiting them. Faith, at times, is only a word, a picture, a dream, an anticipation, *but it is still faith.*

Your loss has devastated your life. It has wiped away the picture of life, the dream on the horizon. Maybe you feel like faith has died, too. Maybe your faith has only been stretched, reshaped, sent off in a new direction, just waiting for you to reach forward and grab it (that's another word for trust). Maybe your spiritual self is more intact than you realize, and your struggle is with religious rituals that seem empty, words that clutter your life with meaninglessness, or the lack of people around to offer even a word of comfort.

Surrender. Turn the hands over. Leave an opening. The Spirit breathes through that opening. It doesn't always come with hurricane force. It sometimes comes gently: a kind word, a prayer spoken aloud that sounds different than before, a devotional reading that was written for thousands of subscribers to a devotional book series, but seems to have your name on it. It's as if someone just knew, and knew you. The minister comes down the communion rail, as he or she has done for months since this grief journey began. Maybe today something happens, a light goes off, and you discover in the words "The Body of Christ" the invitation that enables you to risk the words of the psalmist, "O taste and see that the Lord is good" (Psalm 34:8).

Today could be different at temple. Another worshiper take the time to say hello, to ask your name, to share his story or list to your story. Maybe you took the first move. A stranger becom a friend. Maybe someone else has experienced a loss and you reach out to her. In her face you see your face; in her tears, your tears; in her longing, the sign that you have moved closer to an experience of hope.

Darcie Sims has offered a profound look at hope and faith. I doesn't come from the "ivory palaces" of the theologians, but from the honest yearning of this bereaved parent and bereavement specialist. Her audiocassette set, *If I Could Just See Hope*, meets us as we lament the lack of hope on the horizon, the embi tered emptiness in our hearts. We are then invited by one who knows that journey well, to trust, *to risk* the possibility of hope.

This isn't semantics or game playing. It's about respecting th grief journey and yourself enough to know that time is your bes friend, that everything is filtered through your loss (even faith!), and that you have the right to expect a new horizon, "to hope fc hope." It doesn't work out with a glorious picture on the screen, like in some happy Disney movie. No, it is hope's possibility, often glimpsed, frequently missed, that usually shows up in the least expected places. It is possible. It is real.

Rabbi Earl Grollman said it well in a presentation recently fc hospice workers gathered in Chicago. "Everything in life is a risk—unless you just want to stay home. You have to take the ri in order to survive."

Take the risk. Turn the hands over. Look for God. Look for hope. If that still seems too much for you, just take the risk to lo beyond yourself.

Searching. Looking. I want it worked out, Lord. Heal me. Take aw the pain. I am too angry to move, I can't move these tired hands. I wan to love. I want to hope. I want to heal. Help me to take the risk. Yes, again—or maybe for the first time. Amen.

Postscript

Jacob

Jacob was quite the energetic one. He could see what he wanted and had the energy, the self-serving devotion, to go after it. He wasn't always bad, but he certainly could be very "I" focused. Probably his biggest strength, and thus also his vulnerability, was his conviction that he could "lick" anything or anyone that stood in his way.

So it comes as no surprise that he would encounter a stranger (Genesis 32:22-29) and wrestle him until dawn. We don't know what Jacob was looking for—whether he was out to conquer or, perceiving himself to be threatened, was simply determined to protect himself. In any case the stranger was met, they wrestled, and Jacob seemed to walk away the winner. But was he?

His opponent was God, and Jacob seemed all the better (if measured by his old standards) by winning this match. For those of you who question the existence of God, or wonder if God is really powerless in the face of the world's problems and your sorrows, this story, on the surface, fails to offer any comfort. God is a weakling. Even World Federation Wrestling would have recognized the need for God to win. Anything else would be bad public relations.

But this isn't about public relations, and despite the typical mentality we have about most of life's challenges or contests, it isn't about winning and losing. It is about letting go of self, trusting, believing, becoming both yourself and also a new person. What Jacob won was recognized in his new name, *Israel*, "for you have striven with God and with humans, and have prevailed."

Jacob was stubborn and determined. He seemed to lick another opponent. The real winner, of course, is God. God is both stubborn and determined to love us, to care for us, to gently carry us in his arms, to name us, to claim us, to weep with us, and to lift us up—not by erasing our problems (and discounting our feelings), but by walking us through our valleys and our grief.

Jacob entered his wrestling match with the very same questions we often struggle with. He was asking, "Where am I headed?" "What can I do about my life situation?" and "What does it all

mean for me?" Why? Who? What? When? Those are the sa[me]
questions we are asking, or have asked, or will ask. All of the qu[es]
tions are about relating or connecting.

Jacob forced the will of God. He thought he could take matt[er]
into his own hands. He had all of the answers, all of the expla[na]
tions (although his track record would suggest otherwise). Jac[ob]
shows us how to wrestle, how to know and see a divine presen[ce,]
God, in the ring with us. Jacob didn't walk away with everyth[ing]
worked out. He still knew very little about the todays and tom[or]
rows of his life. I doubt he truly understood the implications of [that]
long night on the ground.

God understood. God stayed with him, was truly present, a[nd]
Jacob realized not his own sense of victory, but the victory of a G[od]
who refused to walk away or abandon him in his valleys, in [the]
vast open spaces of his wanderings, and in his heart. That is wh[at]
brought Jacob to the winner's circle. The circle surrounding hi[m,]
into which he was privileged to walk and stand, was the embra[ce]
of the very God he so long had doubted or schemed against.

We may not be doubters and schemers but, like Jacob, we m[ay]
be trying to force God's hand. "Tell us, God, why you let my ba[by]
die." "Explain to me, God, where you were when the drunk d[ri]
ver…" "What are you doing, God, about all of the violence?" Wh[en]
we raise these questions (and it is okay to do that—don't let an[y]
one tell you otherwise!), we are entering the wrestling match. G[od]
and we are wrestling together. Stay with it. It validates your fe[el]
ings, and will bring comfort in the midst of sorrow.

Jacob walked away with truth, not answers. "For I have se[en]
God face to face…." It was the experience that took over, and t[he]
arena was transformed. Whether our arena is a desert spot, a gy[m]
nasium, our living room, or our bedroom as we weep oursel[ves]
into restless dozing, it—and we—become sacred ground. G[od]
steps in and transforms this space, ourselves, and our sorrow i[nto]
a sacred place where God and we come together.

We still don't have answers. In fact, our list of questions m[ay]
have expanded. But answers seem less important now. What m[at]
ters is that we are back on course. In the impossible wilderness [of]
our sorrow, a sacred place has been discovered. It has become [a]
place with God. At least for a moment in our journey we are l[ess]

ost, and maybe God feels a little less lost—at least from our perpective.

Wrestling. Connections. This is spirituality.

Habakkuk

Habakkuk (1:1-3; 2:1-4) was an official of the religious community, a liturgist in the temple. He knew the language, ritual, and dynamics of the religion and the community. He was clergy, perceived as a holy person with one of those direct lines to God.

But his job description changed. Maybe there was downsizing in the temple. In any case, he was called to switch from liturgist to prophet, from priest to preacher, and he had to see life outside the safe walls of the temple. He had a rude awakening and experienced both a horror that attacked the very fibers of his faith and a sense of futility about it all.

We sometimes have comfortable periods in our lives. Then some event, or maybe a string of events, moves us out from the safe walls of our environment, our homes, our theologies. We are forced to see life as it is, or can be sometimes.

Any death of a loved one leaves a rawness within us that makes us ripe for questions, doubt, and wonder. Wondering leads to wandering, and how many of us know that pathway? I tell religious leaders that all of their inactive members are missing because of a loss of some kind. The leaders don't always understand this. Habakkuk understood.

For him it was confronting the sins of God's people. For you it may be the "stuckness" in your life, a specific loss, a series of losses, or just one of those detours in life that has left you wandering. All of these become crossroads experiences, junctions, as we are forced to examine, evaluate, and make a decision. This is also the process of faith. We have questions. We want answers. We are lost. We want a very specific road map with all of the highway markers clearly circled. We want a lot, but we get what we need.

Habakkuk had doubts. "God, why are you doing this?" was his question, though he offered some different words. He was demanding answers, intervention, and—to use a word common to many of us who have experienced loss—justice. "Make it right,

God, and then everything will be right with me!" It is the timel[e]
cry of the bereaved and others who search for life's meaning. "H[ow]
long, O Lord, have I cried to thee, unanswered?"

There it is—God is not answering our prayers. It is at the he[art]
of the majority of letters, calls, and questions I receive from dee[ply]
hurt, bereaved folks. "I prayed, and I prayed, and I…" "God let [me]
down. I don't pray anymore." "I must really have failed my lov[ed]
one. I should have prayed harder. Then God would have ma[de]
things different. Can you teach me how to pray?"

Those are our questions, as they were the questions plac[ed]
before Jesus by the disciples who marveled at his work and wor[ds].
He taught them the "Our Father," but he really wasn't teachi[ng]
words. He was teaching *relationship*—a relationship built on tr[ust]
and belief (however shaky at times), even when everything see[ms]
to go against us and against God.

We can teach about prayer and how to pray, but those really [are]
process issues that are secondary to the larger issue of relationsh[ip].
When people are bereaved, questioning God and themselves, th[ey]
often fail to see that that very process is a prayer. Prayer isn't ab[out]
words and formulas; it is an expression of relationship. Troubl[ed]
prayer comes from our heart to God's heart.

Since Habakkuk is relatively unknown to us (about all [we]
know is his name and job description), maybe that gives us t[he]
freedom to substitute our names, our stories, our wounds. "Lor[d,]
look around here. Do you see the ruin? The pain? The deep sorro[w?]
How long, O Lord?"

When we are on the grief journey, the last thing we need is [to]
receive a bunch of platitudes, instructions, or shortcuts. None [of]
them works. What we need is a friend to steady us on our cour[se,]
to patiently bring us an awareness of who we are and where we [are]
on this rough ride through loss.

Habakkuk's questions flew away, and there was no change [in]
his job description. What seemed to change, but had always be[en]
there, was the reminder that God was never displeased with hi[m]
and certainly was not distant from his life and struggle. That w[as]
the answered prayer and the affirmed relationship. Habakku[k's]
reply? "I will stand at my watchpost, and station myself on t[he]
rampart; I will keep watch to see what he will say to me, and wh[at]

he will answer concerning my complaint." Watch. Wait. Then the Lord answered.

Patience. Wrestling. Searching. Wandering. Wondering. Still there is connection. This is spirituality.

Andy

Andy was an Episcopal priest from Idaho. I never knew him. I "met" him in a sermon preached by The Right Reverend William Swing, bishop of the (Episcopal) Diocese of California. He was preaching at a special service marking the completion of a major building project, the cathedral Close, and also the tenth anniversary of the ministry of the dean of Grace Cathedral, the Very Reverend Alan Jones.

The story introduced us to Andy, who had come to California from his small town and small parish to a diocese-sponsored continuing education event. After the event he returned to Idaho. Some time later he went fishing. Apparently when docking, some accident occurred, and he disappeared.

After due course, when all searches for the body were exhausted, a funeral was held. Months later, at Grace Cathedral, it was time for the celebration of the Eucharist (the Lord's Supper), and in walked a man. His face and hands were worn and scarred from the weather, the marks of a person abandoned to the streets to find his way. Yet he seemed familiar to some, and seemed to think something looked familiar about this place. As he arrived, the worshipers were in line to receive the sacrament. This "stranger" joined the line and made his communion with God. When the service ended, this strangely familiar man walked to a priest and said, "I don't know who I am, or where I am, but I know that I belong here."

We, too, bear the scars of life's struggles on our hands and in our hearts. A look at the faces of all the bereaved shows what the storms of life can afflict upon us. Who are we? Where are we? Where do we belong?

Here! Connected! Meal. Belonging even when scarred. This is spirituality.

Connections

Spirituality. It has been the frail attempt of this book to off
you some glimpse of what spirituality is, and can be, in your lif
The connections may feel threatened, worn, or twisted and tugge
out, but they are still connections. As you travel this pathway w
call grief, may you be focused on spirituality as connection. It is m
prayer for you (and for me) that you will continue to wrestle, eve
when you feel you have no strength, that you will risk waiting a li
tle longer, and that you will experience communion (which is con
nection), even when you are not sure who you are or where yo
are. That is the pathway to peace, hope, and healing, and those ce
tainly are the gifts that await all of us in grief.

O Lord, support us all the day long of this troublous life, until t
shades lengthen, and the evening comes, and the busy world is hushed, t
fever of life is over, and our work is done. Then, Lord, in your mercy gra
us a safe lodging, a holy rest, and peace at the last. Amen.
—*John Cardinal Newman (1801-189(*

Resources

Resources are important if we are to combat the painful loneliness that often accompanies grief. Because of space limitations, I will offer only resources related to the spiritual aspects of grief. A future book, which will be a grief companion, will offer extensive resources on grief, including books, cassettes, videos, and speakers.

In the meantime, if you have any need for assistance on resources, please feel free to contact us at CONNECTIONS - SPIRITUAL LINKS. We will gladly direct you to the resources that you need. Our extensive bibliographies also include a much more detailed look at the resources available on the subjects of spirituality and grief.

My 'Top Ten' List of Recommended Resources

Booth, Leo, *The God Game: It's Your Move*, Walpole, New Hampshire, Stillpoint, 1994. This book explores the abusive experiences and less helpful understandings of God and spirituality that block our path to healing.

DelZoppo, Patrick, *Mourning: The Journey From Grief to Healing*, Staten Island, New York, Alba House, 1995. A good walk through the grief experience with faith woven all throughout.

Ehrich, Thomas, *Journey; 365 Meditations for People on the Way*, New York, New York, Crossroad, 1995. A wonderfully broad sweep through life and faith.

Fraser, Lyn, *Water From the Rock: Finding Grace in Time of Grief*, New York, New York, Paulist, 1994. A gentle yet persuasive walk through loss, life, and faith.

Grollman, Earl, *What Helped Me When My Loved One Died*, Boston, Massachusetts, Beacon, 1981. Brilliant insights from a comforting friend. There is help.

Miller, James, *A Pilgrimage Through Grief: Healing the Soul's Hu* *After Loss*, **St. Meinrad, Indiana, Abbey Press, 1995.** We experience our Babylon waters of loss with renewed hope and faith.

Mundy, Linus, *Prayer-Walking: A Simple Path to Body-and-Sou* *Fitness*, **St. Meinrad, Indiana, Abbey Press, 1994.** This book wi help you find your path to spiritual fitness.

Shapiro, Rami, *Open Hearts: A Jewish Guide to Comfortin* *Mourners*, **Redmond, Washington, Medic Publishing, 1992** Crosses barriers and boundaries to provide comfort for Jewis mourners and those outside that faith tradition who seek to wal with them.

Sims, Darcie, *If I Could Just See Hope* **(audiocassettes), Wenatche** **Washington, Big A & Company, 1994.** Darcie, truly a remarkabl friend to the bereaved, brings us to a realistic experience of hope' possibility in our lives.

Williams, Philip, *When A Loved One Dies: Meditations for th* *Journey Through Grief*, **Minneapolis, Minnesota, Augsburg, 1995** With words of faith, prayer, and unconditional love, Williams cut to the heart of loss and hope.

In addition to the above ten books, no list would be complete without mentioning *Bereavement* magazine, the best resource and bargain in bereavement caregiving. Contact Andrea Gambill, 8133 Telegraph Drive, Colorado Springs, Colorado, 80920.

About the Author

The Reverend Richard B. Gilbert, M.Div., FAAGC, CPBC, is the founding director of CONNECTIONS - SPIRITUAL LINKS. A bereavement specialist, he brings extensive experience as a chaplain, educator, author and reviewer, plus his own grief journey, to this book. A regular columnist in *Bereavement* magazine, he is an author and spokesperson for One Caring Place/Abbey Press, a conference presenter, resource person, and a partner in the Hope For Bereaved - National Bereavement Center (315-475-9675), which handles his bookings and programs.